Halle Berry

Julia Holt

Published in association with The Basic Skills Agency

Hodder & Stoughton
A MEMBER OF THE HODDER HEADLINE GROUP

Acknowledgements
Cover: Michael Williams/London Features International/UWIL

Photos: p. 2 © R. Hepler/Everett/REX FEATURES; p. 5 © AP Photo/Dave Caulkin; p. 12 © BFI Stills; p. 15 © Star Traks/REX FEATURES; p. 18 © BFI Stills; p. 22 © Chris Weeks/BEI/REX FEATURES; p. 27 © PA Photos/EPA.

Orders; please contact Bookpoint Ltd, 130 Milton Park, Abingdon, Oxon OX14 4SB. Telephone (44) 01235 827720, Fax: (44) 01235 400454. Lines are open from 9.00–6.00, Monday to Saturday, with a 24 hour message answering service. You can also order through our website www.hodderheadline.co.uk

British Library Cataloguing in Publication Data
A catalogue record for this title is available from the British Library

ISBN 0 340 87653 0

First published 2003
Impression number   10 9 8 7 6 5 4 3 2 1
Year   2007 2006 2005 2004 2003

Typeset by SX Composing DTP, Rayleigh, Essex.
Printed in Great Britain for Hodder & Stoughton Educational, a division of Hodder Headline, 338 Euston Road, London NW1 3BH by The Bath Press, Bath.

Contents

1 Halle: Introduction

Halle Berry has worked hard
to show Hollywood
that she is more than just a pretty face.
She has proved it
over and over again.
Now she is one of the biggest stars
in Hollywood.

Halle was a beautiful baby
and she grew up
to be a beautiful woman.
She was a beauty contest winner
and the 'face' of Revlon cosmetics.
She has also found the time
to win an Oscar.

Halle Berry has strength as well as beauty.

But life has not always been easy.
Halle has faced illness, divorce
and violence.
All of these have made her
a stronger person.

2 The Early Years

Halle was born
on 14 August 1968,
in Cleveland, Ohio.

She was named after
a local department store,
Halle Brothers.

Halle and her big sister
were raised by their mum,
who was a nurse.
Their dad drank a lot
and wasn't at home much.

Halle, aged 20 in Ohio

Halle's father left the family
when Halle was four years old
and only came back
to beat them up.

Violence is her first memory.
Halle has no contact with her dad
to this day.

Being the mixed-race child
of a single mum
gave Halle a lot of problems.

When they lived in an all-black area
the other kids were mean to her
because she had light skin
and straight hair.

Then they moved to an all-white area.
There the other kids were mean
because she was beautiful.

3 The Beauty Queen

All of this made
Halle try harder at school.
She became the editor
of her school paper
and a cheer-leader.

Then she was chosen to be Queen of the Prom.
The other children said that she cheated
so she had to share the prize
with a white girl.

But she put it all behind her
and went on to win beauty contests
like Miss Teen America
and Miss Ohio.
Then Halle was first runner-up
in the Miss USA contest in 1986.

In a few years
she had won enough money
to go to college.

So that's what she did.
She went to Chicago
to learn about acting and
to learn how to write for newspapers.

In 1989, the doctors told Halle
that she was a diabetic.
But she was strong enough
to cope with the news.
She just kept on working.

4 First Film . . . First Wedding

Her big break came in 1991.
First, she was given
a part in a serious film.
She played a drug addict, called Vivian,
in the film *Jungle Fever*.

Then, she had a part in a
TV soap opera.
It was called *Knot's Landing*.
Halle played the part of
Debbie Porter for two years.

Halle in *The Flintstones* in 1994.

For the next few years
Halle worked with famous actors
like Eddie Murphy and Bruce Willis.
She made films like *The Flintstones*.

But she became more famous
for stories about her
in the newspapers.
In the past she chose
the wrong men as boyfriends.
One man beat her up so badly
that she lost her hearing
in one ear.

So, when she asked
David Justice to marry her
everyone was happy.
He was a famous baseball player.
He played for the Atlanta Braves.

Halle and David
had only known each other
for six months
when they got married.

Halle Berry and David Justice.

It was a fairy-tale wedding.
Their photos were in all the newspapers.

But in less than three years
Halle divorced David.
It was a very bad time
and she had to use the police
to protect her.

5 The Award Winner

Again she threw herself into work.
This time for charity.
She went to Sarajevo
to support the troops.
She also worked to support
cancer charities.
Halle was so good at charity work
that she won an award for it.

Halle playing Storm in *X-Men*.

Halle Berry's life
has had big highs and big lows.
The year 2000 was a good example
of both.

First, she won a Golden Globe Award
for her work on TV.

She also won an Emmy
for her role as
Dorothy Dandridge in the film
Introducing Dorothy Dandridge.

Then she starred in *X-Men.*
It is a film based on the comic book stories.
She plays the mutant superhero, Storm.

Best of all she met a new love.
His name is Eric Benet
and he is a singer.
They met when she went to watch
him sing.
They got engaged in 2000.
Halle set up home with
Eric and his little girl, India.

6 In the News

But then tragedy struck.
Halle was in a car crash.
She was driving home
at 2.30 in the morning
when she crashed into another car
at some traffic lights in Hollywood.

She didn't stop
and so the police said
it was a hit-and-run incident.

Halle said she didn't remember the crash.
But she had a big gash on her head
when she got home.
She had to have twenty stitches
in the wound.

Halle with Eric Benet in 2002.

The court gave her three years probation.
She also had to spend 300 hours
carrying out community service
and pay a $13,500 fine.
She still can't remember the crash.

It was a much better year in 2001.
Halle starred as Ginger in *Swordfish*
with John Travolta.
She was paid $2,500,000 for her work.

Also that year,
Halle and Eric got married.
It wasn't a big Hollywood wedding.
It was a quiet wedding in LA.
Then they went on honeymoon
for two weeks
to an island near India.
They want to have a baby
as soon as possible.

7 The Oscar Winner

In 2002, Halle became a
world-wide star.
She was the first
African-American actress
to win the Oscar for best actress.

She won the Oscar
for her part in the film *Monster's Ball*.
It's a very tragic and violent film.
Halle plays a woman whose son is killed.
She meets a man whose son
was also killed.
They fall in love
and then they find out
that they have other tragedies in common.

Halle was so happy
to win the Oscar.
She had made history.

She said,
'It was about being
the first black woman,
but now I hope
I'm on my way
to being just Halle Berry,
the actress,
not always being black first.'

Halle accepts her Oscar in 2002.

The year 2002 ended with Halle
being the latest Bond girl.
In *Die Another Day*.
She plays the part of Jinx.
But is she a goody or a baddy?
You will have to see the film
yourself to find out!

Halle Berry is on her way
to being known by her name
and not just as a beautiful face.

She has proved beyond a doubt
that she can act
and she is a big star.